Farm Pets

Happy Horses

Colleen Dolphin
AUTHOR

C.A. Nobens
ILLUSTRATOR

Consulting Editor, Diane Craig, M.A./Reading Specialist

ABDO
Publishing Company

Published by ABDO Publishing Company, 8000 West 78th Street, Edina, Minnesota 55439.

Copyright © 2011 by Abdo Consulting Group, Inc. International copyrights reserved in all countries.

No part of this book may be reproduced in any form without written permission from the publisher. SandCastle™ is a trademark and logo of ABDO Publishing Company.

Printed in the United States of America, North Mankato, Minnesota
052010
092010

 PRINTED ON RECYCLED PAPER

Editor: Liz Salzmann
Content Developer: Nancy Tuminelly
Cover and Interior Design and Production: Colleen Dolphin, Mighty Media
Photo Credits: iStockphoto (Robert Churchill), Shutterstock

Library of Congress Cataloging-in-Publication Data
Dolphin, Colleen, 1979-
 Happy horses / Colleen Dolphin.
   p. cm. -- (Farm pets)
 ISBN 978-1-61613-372-6
 1. Horses--Juvenile literature. I. Title.
 SF302.D65 2010
 636.1--dc22
                          2009053103

SandCastle™ Level: Transitional

SandCastle™ books are created by a team of professional educators, reading specialists, and content developers around five essential components—phonemic awareness, phonics, vocabulary, text comprehension, and fluency—to assist young readers as they develop reading skills and strategies and increase their general knowledge. All books are written, reviewed, and leveled for guided reading, early reading intervention, and Accelerated Reader® programs for use in shared, guided, and independent reading and writing activities to support a balanced approach to literacy instruction. The SandCastle™ series has four levels that correspond to early literacy development. The levels are provided to help teachers and parents select appropriate books for young readers.

Emerging Readers (no flags)   Beginning Readers (1 flag)   Transitional Readers (2 flags)   Fluent Readers (3 flags)

SandCastle™ would like to hear from you. Please send us your comments and suggestions.
sandcastle@abdopublishing.com

Contents

Horses

Horses are **exciting** pets. They love to **graze** and **gallop**. A horse can take you for a ride!

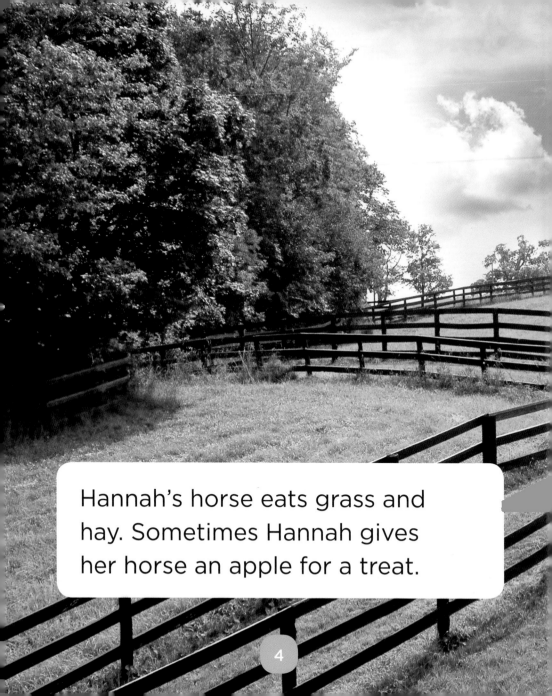

Hannah's horse eats grass and hay. Sometimes Hannah gives her horse an apple for a treat.

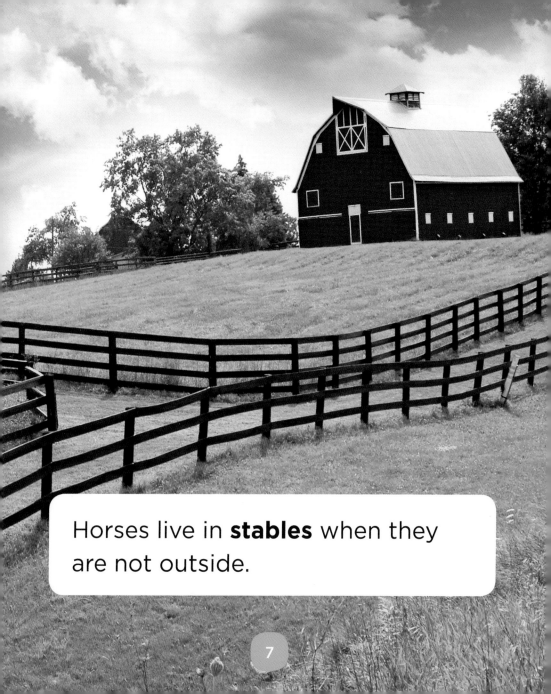

Horses live in **stables** when they are not outside.

Horses need exercise. Al takes his horse riding every day.

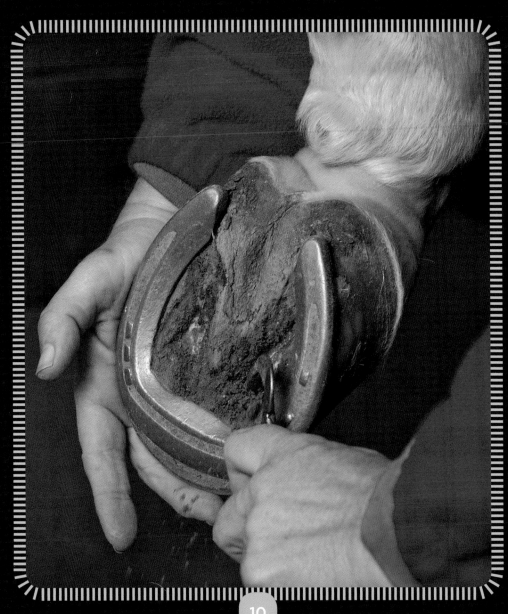

Jess cleans her horse's hooves when they get dirty.

Horses need to drink a lot of water.

A Horse Story

Michael has a fast
horse named Ace.
He wants to ride Ace
in the yearly race.

Michael and Ace run
and jump all day long.
Ace eats lots of hay
to keep him strong.

Finally the morning of the big race arrives. Ace rides in his **trailer** as Michael's dad drives.

Michael and Ace are ready
for the race to begin.
They have a lot of fun
and finish for the win!

Did You Know?

* Horses sleep for about three hours a day.

* Horses usually sleep standing up. They only lie down to sleep every few days.

* Horses are called *foals* until they are one year old.

* The left side of a horse is called the *near side*. The right side is called the *off side*.

Horse Quiz

Read each sentence below. Then decide whether it is true or false!

1. Horses live in **stables**.

2. Horses do not need exercise.

3. Horse's hooves should be cleaned when they get dirty.

4. Horses need a lot of water.

5. Michael and Ace lose the race.

Answers: 1. True   2. False   3. True   4. True   5. False

Glossary

exciting – causing eagerness or happiness.

gallop – the fastest speed a horse can run.

graze – to eat grasses and plants.

stable – a building, such as a barn, where animals live and eat.

trailer – a large cart with walls and a roof that is pulled by a car or truck.

To see a complete list of SandCastle™ books and other nonfiction titles from ABDO Publishing Company, visit www.abdopublishing.com.

8000 West 78th Street, Edina, MN 55439 • 800-800-1312 • fax 952-831-1632